From Offer to Ownership

The Modern Home Buyer's Guide

John Graff

ELLIMAT BOOKS

Ellimat Books

ISBN: 979-8-9852750-4-9 **(paperback)**

Although the advice and information in this book are believed to be accurate and true as of the time of publication, neither the authors nor the publisher can accept any legal responsibility or liability for any inaccuracies or any loss, harm, or injury that comes about from following instructions or advice in the book.

First Edition published by Ellimat Books 2023

Dedication

All my love and gratitude to Matt, Elliott, and Cuth-
bert.

Contents

Chapter 1

Introduction to Home Buying

Welcome, future homeowner! Embarking on the path to purchasing a home is an exciting adventure. For many, it marks a significant milestone, whether it's achieving a personal dream, setting down roots for a family, or making a sound financial investment. But like any adventure, it comes with its twists, turns, and unique challenges.

The Journey Ahead: What to Expect

The home buying journey is multifaceted. It involves more than just choosing a house and signing a contract. You'll be making several crucial decisions – from understanding mortgages to negotiating prices, and from inspecting properties to, finally, turning the key in your new front door. While it might seem daunting, remember that countless individuals and families have walked this path before you. And with the right knowledge, you'll not only survive this journey, but you'll thrive.

Benefits of Homeownership

So, why do millions choose to buy homes every year? Homeownership, for many, is more than just a financial decision; it's a milestone symbolizing achievement and stability. One of the most tangible benefits homeowners experience is the ability to build equity as they pay down their mortgage. This equity often grows as real estate typically appreciates over time, turning the home into a valuable asset. Additionally, with a fixed-rate mortgage, homeowners have the added advantage of predictable monthly payments, offering a shield against the unpredictable surges in rent that many renters face. Financial benefits also extend to tax breaks, where homeowners may have opportunities to deduct mortgage interest and property taxes, translating to potential annual savings.

Yet, the allure of homeownership isn't just fiscal. The autonomy of owning a space is liberating. Homeowners can personalize, renovate, and adapt their homes to their evolving tastes and needs without seeking permissions typical in rental situations. This freedom also fosters a deeper connection to one's living environment and often extends to the broader community. As homeowners engage with their neighbors, local schools, and events, there's a palpable sense of belonging and rootedness that's hard to achieve in transient rental settings.

This permanence isn't just about community ties; it also offers homeowners long-term cost efficiency. While the initial investment can be steep, in the long run, owning often proves more economical than renting, especially when factoring in the growth in home equity and the potential for earning rental income, should homeowners choose to lease out their space. Moreover, there's an emotional richness to owning a home—it's a space that can be passed down through generations, and there's profound satisfaction in the knowledge that it's truly yours. This emotional facet, combined with the financial and community aspects, makes homeownership a deeply layered and beneficial endeavor.

There's a Reason Why Homeownership is So Coveted

Equity Building: Unlike paying rent, with every mortgage payment, you build equity in your home. Over time, as you pay down your loan, this equity grows, and your home often appreciates in value.

Stability: Owning a home provides stability. You have the control over your living space, and there's no worry about a landlord increasing the rent or asking you to vacate.

Tax Advantages: In many countries, including the United States, homeowners can enjoy significant tax benefits. This could include deductions on mortgage interest or property taxes. It's essential to consult with a tax professional to understand potential tax benefits in your area.

Creative Freedom: Want to paint your bedroom a deep, dark purple? Or perhaps you're thinking of a complete kitchen remodel? As a homeowner, you have the freedom to make your space truly yours, tailoring it to your tastes without needing permission from a landlord.

Financial Predictability: With a fixed-rate mortgage, you can expect consistent monthly payments, allowing for better financial planning and management. Rent, on the other hand, might increase over time.

Long-term Investment: Real estate, in most cases, appreciates over time. By purchasing a home, you're making a long-term investment that could yield substantial returns in the future.

Sense of Community: Owning a home often leads to a deeper connection with your neighborhood and community. There's a sense of permanence and be-longing that can be truly fulfilling.

While the benefits of homeownership are numerous, it's also a significant responsibility. There will be un-expected challenges and costs, from repairs to mainte-nance. However, with due diligence, preparation, and the right mindset, these challenges can be managed.

As you delve deeper into this guide, remember that knowledge is power. The more informed you are, the smoother your journey will be. Each chapter is de-signed to equip you with the tools and insights you need to navigate the home buying process with confi-dence.

Ready to begin? Let's take the first step together on this exciting journey to homeownership.

Chapter 2

Understanding Your Finances

U nderstanding your finances when buying a home is akin to charting a course before embarking on a voyage. The journey to homeownership is dotted with numerous challenges and obstacles, many of which are financial. At the outset, it's not just about knowing if you can afford the mortgage payments, but it encompasses a myriad of other costs, from down payments and closing costs to maintenance and property taxes.

Delving deep into one's financial health provides a clearer picture of what one can truly afford. It's essential to assess your monthly income, ongoing expenses, existing debts, and savings. This financial introspection ensures that when you commit to a mortgage, it doesn't become a crushing burden, but rather a manageable responsibility. A comprehensive financial understanding also helps identify how much wiggle room exists for unexpected expenses, which are often part and parcel of homeownership.

Furthermore, understanding your credit score is paramount. This three-digit number can significantly impact the interest rates offered on a mortgage, which over the span of years, can amount to a considerable sum. A robust credit score can open doors to better mortgage deals, whereas a low score might necessitate higher down payments or even result in declined applications.

It's also crucial to anticipate future financial changes. Will there be significant expenses in the near future? Perhaps educational costs, a career change, or potential expansions to the family? Factoring in these changes helps in determining the affordability of a home in the long run, ensuring sustainable homeownership.

In essence, diving deep into one's financial situation is foundational to the home buying process. It safeguards against potential pitfalls and provides the confidence and clarity to make informed decisions. After all, a home is not just a property; it's an investment, a sanctuary, and a testament to one's financial acumen and foresight.

Determining Your Budget

Before embarking on house tours and imagining Sunday mornings in a new home, ascertain what you can realistically afford. Here's a detailed breakdown:

Review Your Monthly Income:

- **Salaried Individuals:** Your monthly budget is straightforward – it's primarily your take-home pay after tax deductions.

- **Freelancers/Contractors:** As incomes can fluctuate, calculate an average monthly income based on the last year. Always err on the side of caution, anticipating potential dry spells.

- **Additional Income:** Don't forget bonuses, rental incomes, dividends, or any other occasional inflows.

Understand Your Expenses:

- **Fixed Costs:** These include rent or existing mortgage payments, car payments, insurance premiums, and other recurring bills.

- **Variable Costs:** Utilities, groceries, dining out, entertainment, and miscellaneous shopping. Analyze bank and credit card statements for the past few months to estimate an average.

- **Savings & Investments:** Money set aside for retirement, emergencies, or other savings goals.

Calculate Debt-to-Income Ratio (DTI): Lenders look at this crucial metric. It's the sum of all your monthly debt payments divided by your gross monthly income. The resulting percentage helps lenders assess your ability to manage monthly payments. A DTI of 36% or less is generally seen favorably, though some lenders allow for higher.

Consider Future Expenses: Buying a home isn't a singular event; it's a long-term commitment. Consider how your financial situation might evolve. Are you planning significant life events, such as a wedding, childbirth, or further education?

Factor in Additional Home Buying Costs: Apart from the home price, remember costs like down payment, closing costs, property taxes, homeowner's insurance, and potential immediate home repairs.

The Importance of Credit Scores and How to Improve Yours

Your credit score can make or break your home-buying dreams. It's essential to understand its significance and work on improving it if necessary.

Why Credit Scores Matter:A high credit score often translates to lower interest rates, which can save you substantial amounts over the life of a loan. Conversely, a lower score can result in higher rates or even loan rejection.

Improving Your Credit Score:

- Consistent Bill Payments: Ensure all bills, especially credit cards and loans, are paid on or before due dates.

- Limit Outstanding Debt: High credit card balances can adversely impact your score. Aim to utilize less than 30% of your available credit.

- Avoid Frequent New Credit Applications: Each hard inquiry can shave points off your score.

- Regularly Monitor and Dispute Errors: Obtain free annual credit reports, review them, and promptly address any inaccuracies.

By following these tips, you can improve your chances of getting approved for a mortgage and buying the home of your dreams.

Saving for a Down Payment: Tips and Tricks

A substantial down payment can make your home buying journey smoother, as it can lead to better mortgage terms and lower monthly payments.

Here are some tips and tricks to help you save for a down payment with the full understanding that not all of these are possible for everyone:

- **Determine the Required Amount**: Traditional advice suggests saving 20% of the home's price. However, various loan types might allow for less. Understand what you're aiming for.

- **Open a Dedicated Savings Account**: Separate your down payment fund from everyday spending to reduce the temptation to dip into it.

- **Automate Transfers**: Schedule automatic transfers post-payday to ensure consistency.

- **Cut Non-essential Spending**: Even small luxuries add up. Consider if there are areas where you can temporarily cut back.

- **Look for Additional Income Sources**: Seasonal jobs, freelancing, or selling unneeded items can give your savings a significant boost.

- **Get a Part-Time Job**: If you have a full-time job, consider getting a part-time job to supplement your income.

- **Sell Unneeded Items**: Go through your belongings and sell anything you don't use or need. This could include clothes, furniture, electronics, and more.

- **Downsize Your Home**: If you have a large home, consider downsizing to a smaller home or apartment. This will free up more money that you can put towards your down payment.

- **Get a Roommate**: If you're single, consider getting a roommate to help you pay your rent. This will free up more money that you can put towards your down payment.

- **Move in with Family or Friends**: If you're able to, consider moving in with family or friends for a period of time. This will save you money on rent, which you can then put towards your down payment.

Saving for a down payment can be a challenge, but it's definitely possible with hard work and dedication. By following these tips and tricks, you can reach your goal of owning a home sooner rather than later.

Here are some additional tips:

- **Get pre-approved for a mortgage**: This will give you an idea of how much you can afford to borrow and will help you stay on track with your savings.

- **Shop around for the best mortgage rates**: There are many different lenders out there, so it's important to compare rates and terms before you choose one.

- **Be patient**: Saving for a down payment takes time, so don't get discouraged if it doesn't happen overnight. Just keep at it and you'll eventually reach your goal.

Chapter 3

Recognizing the Right Time: Are You Ready to Buy a Home?

Opting to buy a home stands as a monumental juncture in anyone's life journey. Although the financial facets of this decision are undeniably central—and will receive thorough scrutiny in subsequent chapters—the layers of homeownership delve deeper than just monetary considerations. Often intangible, yet striking a deep chord within us, are factors like our personal ambitions, prevailing lifestyle dynamics, and the future we envision for ourselves and our families. Truly understanding if you're poised to take this significant step is less about a cursory glance at your finances and more about a profound reflection, looking ahead with clarity, and truly grasping where you want your life's path to lead.

Personal Stability and The Spectrum of Commitment:

Homeownership isn't a fleeting affair; it's a profound commitment that often spans large chunks of one's life. Before diving in, it's essential to introspect on your current life stage. Can you visualize yourself firmly anchored in the same locale for several years or even decades? If your horizon potentially includes significant shifts, such as career moves or geographic relocations, a measured approach might be in order. It's about gauging not just where you stand today but forecasting your journey in the years to come.

The Quest for Personalization and Autonomy:

There's an undeniable allure in the freedom home-ownership promises. If you've ever felt stifled by the constraints of rental agreements or dreamt of molding a space to mirror your essence, these are more than whimsical desires. They signal a readiness to own and curate a space. A home, in its truest sense, is more than a structure; it's a canvas awaiting your unique touch.

Anticipating Evolving Needs:

Perhaps today's studio apartment fits your current lifestyle snugly. But what of tomorrow? As life un-furls, introducing new relationships, family expan-sions, or even just evolving dreams, your spatial needs will shift. Owning a home provides the flexibility to grow, adapt, and redefine spaces as per the changing rhythms of life.

From Temporary Spaces to Lasting Foundations:

Renting, while convenient, often feels transient. Over time, there's a growing realization that the funds channeled into rent could gradually build equity in a space truly your own. If you're at this crossroads, where you're keen to transition from ephemeral lodgings to a lasting foundation, it's a poignant sign of your readiness to own.

Yearning for Community Roots:

A home is more than four walls; it's a gateway to a community. Owning a property often translates to deeper community ties, richer local engagements, and lasting neighborhood bonds. If your heart seeks this depth of connection, where you're not just an occupant but an integral community member, your emotional compass is pointing towards homeownership.

Embracing Home Responsibilities:

Every home, like a living entity, needs care and attention. This nurturing goes beyond occasional cleanings, delving into maintenance, timely repairs, and proactive upkeep. A genuine willingness, even eagerness, to embrace these responsibilities speaks volumes about your readiness to own and cherish a home.

The decision to buy a home is multi-dimensional, blending both logic and emotion. While finances are a critical pillar, the journey is enriched by myriad other factors that demand reflection and insight. As you stand at this crossroads, harmonizing your present realities with future aspirations will illuminate the path to a decision that's not just pragmatic but also deeply enriching.

Chapter 4

Recognizing the Right Time: Is The Market Ready For You to Buy?

The realm of real estate is as vast and varied as the landscapes our homes are built upon. It's a world constantly in motion, responding to a confluence of factors like economic shifts, changes in housing needs, and broader societal developments. Picture it as a large puzzle where each piece—from interest rates to urban development policies, from population growth to technological advancements—affects the larger picture of property buying and selling.

Central to understanding this puzzle, especially for those poised on the brink of a property transaction, is the knowledge of two key market conditions: the buyer's market and the seller's market. These aren't just jargon thrown around by real estate professionals; they represent tangible market states that can greatly sway the balance of power in a transaction.

These terms, while straightforward on the surface, are rooted in deeper economic and social dynamics. They don't just dictate pricing but influence everything from negotiation tactics to marketing strategies and even the mood and optimism of buyers and sellers. This chapter aims to demystify these concepts, providing clarity on their differences, and helping you understand how they could shape your real estate journey.

Definition:

Buyer's Market: This is characterized by a surplus of properties available for sale and a shortage of potential buyers. In such a scenario, buyers have the upper hand as they often have a variety of options to choose from, which can lead to more competitive prices.

Seller's Market: Conversely, a seller's market has a high demand for properties but a limited number of homes available for sale. Here, sellers can often ask for higher prices and might receive multiple offers, giving them the advantage.

Pricing Dynamics:

Buyer's Market: With more homes available than buyers, properties might remain on the market for longer durations. This can lead sellers to reduce their asking prices, providing buyers with the opportunity to negotiate better deals.

Seller's Market: The scarcity of listings drives prices up. Homes are likely to sell quickly, sometimes even above the asking price, especially if multiple buyers are vying for the same property.

Negotiation Power:

Buyer's Market: Buyers often have more room to negotiate terms, contingencies, and prices. They can request repairs, ask the seller to cover closing costs, or even get a favorable move-in date.

Seller's Market: Sellers wield more influence. They're less likely to make concessions or entertain lowball offers. In fact, bidding wars can sometimes erupt, pushing buyers to offer more than they initially intended.

Time on the Market:

Buyer's Market: Homes can sit on the market for extended periods. If a property is listed for a long time, it might hint at overpricing or other underlying issues.

Seller's Market: Properties sell rapidly. It's not uncommon for homes to receive offers within days, or even hours, of being listed.

Implications for Strategy:

Buyer's Market: Buyers should take their time to explore options, research neighborhoods, and inspect properties. They have the leverage to be choosy and negotiate favorable terms.

Seller's Market: Sellers should focus on presentation and curb appeal to maximize returns. Meanwhile, buyers should be decisive, pre-approved for mortgages, and ready to act swiftly to secure a property.

Understanding whether the current market leans towards buyers or sellers is crucial in shaping one's approach to real estate transactions. Whether you're looking to buy your dream home or sell an existing property, being aware of these dynamics can help you make informed decisions, set realistic expectations, and navigate the process more efficiently.

Chapter 5

Getting Pre-approved for a Mortgage

So, you have your finances in order, and you have a clear understanding of your budget. The next big step on this home buying journey is securing a mortgage. Before you begin house hunting in earnest, getting pre-approved for a mortgage can provide clarity on what you can afford and show sellers that you are a serious buyer.

Getting pre-approved for a mortgage when buying a home is a critical step, serving as both a practical guide and a strategic advantage in the home-buying process. Think of it as a financial passport, signaling to all parties involved—realtors, sellers, and even yourself—just how prepared you are to make a purchase.

Firstly, a mortgage pre-approval provides clarity. Before diving into the vast ocean of home listings, it's pivotal to know how deep your pockets go. A pre-approval outlines precisely how much a lender is willing to offer, grounding your search in reality. Instead of aimlessly wandering through homes that might be beyond reach or underselling your capacity, you'll be able to target properties that align with your financial bandwidth.

This leads to the second advantage: efficiency. Time is of the essence in hot real estate markets. By being pre-approved, you can act swiftly when you find a home that resonates with you. Sellers often receive multiple offers, especially if the property is in a prime location or priced attractively. Having a pre-approval signals to the seller that you're not only serious but also financially vetted. This can give you an edge over other potential buyers who might be waiting on their financial clearances.

Additionally, the pre-approval process can shine a light on potential credit issues that might need addressing. If there are discrepancies or areas of concern in your credit history, it's far better to know and address them upfront rather than facing unpleasant surprises after finding your dream home.

Moreover, understanding the parameters of your pre-approved mortgage can help in negotiations. Armed with this knowledge, you can confidently negotiate prices, knowing your upper limit and staying within a comfortable range.

In essence, obtaining a mortgage pre-approval ensures that your home-buying journey is anchored in financial realism, bolsters your credibility in the eyes of sellers, and fine-tunes your search, making the entire process more streamlined and less stressful.

Different Types of Mortgages Explained

The world of mortgages can be complex. Each mortgage type offers its own benefits and considerations. Here's a rundown:

Fixed-Rate Mortgages: A mortgage where the interest rate remains the same throughout the entire life of the loan.

- Pros: Monthly payments are stable, making it easier to budget. Excellent if current rates are low.

- Cons: Interest rates might be higher than initial adjustable-rate mortgages.

Adjustable-Rate Mortgages (ARMs): Interest rates can change periodically depending on changes in a corresponding financial index.

- Pros: Typically offer a lower initial rate than fixed-rate mortgages.

- Cons: Monthly payment can increase, sometimes significantly, when rates adjust.

Federal Government-Backed Mortgages: Examples include FHA, VA, and USDA loans.

- **Pros:** Often require lower down payments and are more forgiving of lower credit scores.

- **Cons:** Might have specific eligibility requirements and limits on loan amounts.

Jumbo Mortgages: For home loans that exceed federal loan limits.

- **Pros:** Can finance larger, more expensive homes.

- **Cons:** Stricter credit requirements and higher down payments.

The Pre-approval Process and Its Importance

Why Pre-approval?

- **Strengthens Your Position:** Sellers prefer buyers who are pre-approved, as it shows you have the financial capability to purchase the home.

- **Budget Clarity:** Helps narrow down your home search to properties within your loan approval range.

- **Price Negotiations:** Gives you a better standing during price negotiations.

Steps to Pre-approval:

1. Gather Necessary Documentation: This usually includes proof of income (recent pay stubs, tax returns), proof of assets (bank statements, retirement accounts), credit history, and any other relevant financial information.

2. Choose a Lender: Research multiple lenders, considering both interest rates and customer service reviews.

3. Submit an Application: The lender will thoroughly review your financial situation and determine if (and for how much) you qualify.

4. Receive Pre-approval Letter: This letter indicates the amount the lender is willing to loan and the mortgage rate.

Note: Pre-approval doesn't mean you're committed to a loan; it's an indication of what you qualify
for. When you decide on a house, you'll need to go
through the full mortgage application process.

Shopping for the Best Mortgage Rates

Mortgage rates can vary significantly between lenders.
Even a small difference in the rate can result in thou-
sands saved over the lifespan of the loan. Here's how
to get the best rates:

Research Multiple Lenders: Don't just go with the
first lender you come across. Shop around.

Understand Rate Locks: A rate lock guarantees a
certain interest rate for a specified period, protecting
you from potential rate increases during your home
search.

Check Your Credit Score Again: The better your
score, the better your rate. Ensure no errors have
cropped up and negatively impacted your score.

Consider Points: Mortgage points are upfront fees you pay the lender to reduce your interest rate. It can be worth it if you plan to stay in the house for a long time.

Armed with a pre-approval and an understanding of mortgages, you're in a prime position to begin your home search with confidence. Not only will you have a clearer picture of your budget, but sellers will view you as a serious buyer, giving you an edge in any negotiations. Up next, we'll delve into the role of real estate agents and how to find the right one for you.

Chapter 6

Finding the Right Real Estate Agent

Venturing into the world of real estate can be overwhelming. While the Internet offers a plethora of listings and virtual tours, there's an undeniable value in having a knowledgeable professional by your side. A real estate agent not only streamlines the process but can also provide insights that aren't readily available to the general public. The right real estate agent serves as an invaluable ally, guiding clients through this labyrinth with expertise, negotiating prowess, and market insight. Finding the right agent, however, is an endeavor in itself, one that merits careful consideration and research.

One of the foundational aspects of finding a fitting agent is aligning with someone who understands your unique needs and goals. Real estate isn't just about brick and mortar; it's deeply personal, intertwined with one's aspirations, financial standing, and future plans. A suitable agent will take the time to understand these aspects, tailoring their approach to align with your objectives.

Experience and local expertise are vital. While an agent might have numerous sales under their belt, it's essential to ascertain their familiarity with the specific area or market segment you're interested in. Local agents bring insights about neighborhoods, schools, public transport, future developments, and even the micro-trends that might not be immediately apparent in broader market data.

Communication is key. The home buying or selling process can be riddled with complexities and, at times, unexpected twists. Having an agent who communicates proactively, clarifies doubts, and keeps you updated about progress is crucial. The frequency, mode, and clarity of communication can significantly influence the overall experience.

Additionally, consider the agent's network. Real estate isn't an isolated industry. From home inspectors and mortgage brokers to contractors and legal professionals, an agent's network can ease various stages of the transaction. An agent with a robust professional network can offer recommendations and connections that might streamline the process.

Lastly, it's always advisable to seek referrals and reviews. Past clients can offer candid insights about their experience with the agent. While online reviews provide a broad perspective, personal referrals can delve into specific experiences, offering a more nuanced understanding of the agent's approach and efficacy.

In essence, finding the right real estate agent is a blend of research, alignment of goals, and personal rapport. This partnership, when forged with care, can demystify the complexities of real estate, turning a potentially stressful endeavor into a rewarding journey.

Why You Need a Real Estate Agent

Local Market Knowledge: Real estate agents have their finger on the pulse of local markets. They can advise on the right neighborhoods, upcoming developments, and even school districts.

Negotiation Skills: An experienced agent can help you navigate the negotiation process, ensuring you get the best price possible.

Connections: From home inspectors to mortgage brokers, agents have a network of professionals that can expedite and simplify various aspects of the home buying process.

Paperwork & Legalities: The home buying process involves a mound of paperwork. Agents are familiar with all the forms, reports, and other necessary documents, reducing the chances of costly mistakes.

Saves Time and Stress: An agent can filter out unsuitable listings, set up viewings, and answer questions, freeing up your time and reducing the stress associated with house hunting.

How to Choose the Right Agent

Finding the right agent is crucial. You'll be entrusting them with one of the most significant financial transactions of your life. Here are steps to ensure you make a wise choice:

Seek Recommendations: Begin by asking friends, family, and colleagues for their recommendations. Personal experiences can offer invaluable insights.

Check Online Reviews: Websites like Zillow, Realtor.com, and Yelp can provide reviews and feedback on different agents.

Interview Multiple Agents: Before settling on an agent, interview at least three. This gives you a perspective on different working styles, strategies, and personalities.

Ask the Right Questions: During the interview:

- What's their experience in the local market?

- How many clients do they currently have?

- Do they work full-time as an agent?

- What's their strategy for helping you find the right home within your budget?

- Can they provide references?

Assess Their Availability: A good agent should be readily accessible, responsive, and attentive to your needs.

Understand the Commission Structure: Typically, the seller pays the commission, which is then split between the listing agent and the buyer's agent. Ensure you're clear on any costs that might come your way.

The Role of a Buyer's Agent vs. a Listing Agent

It's essential to understand the distinction between a buyer's agent and a listing agent:

- **Buyer's Agent:** Represents you, the buyer. Their primary role is to protect your interests, guide you through the buying process, and help you secure a home at the best possible price and terms.

- **Listing Agent:** Represents the seller. Their primary responsibility is to market the property and get the best price and terms for the seller.

While it's possible to buy a home without an agent or by using the listing agent, having a dedicated buyer's agent ensures that someone is advocating solely for your interests.

Securing a skilled and trustworthy real estate agent can make the difference between a smooth, successful home buying experience and a tumultuous one. They're not just there to open doors for viewings; they're there to guide, advise, and protect you every step of the way. With the right agent by your side, you're well on your way to finding your dream home. In the next chapter, we'll dive deep into the home search process.

Chapter 7

Embarking on Your Home Search

Now, with a comprehensive understanding of your financial landscape and the right real estate agent at your side, it's time to immerse yourself in the thrilling process of house hunting. This chapter will guide you through the intricacies of the search, ensuring you approach it with purpose, clarity, and excitement. Initiating the search often begins long before you physically view properties. It starts with introspection. Identifying what you seek in a home — whether it's a sunlit patio, proximity to work or schools, or a quiet neighborhood — helps streamline the search. While some preferences stem from aesthetic desires, others are rooted in daily life necessities. Balancing the two ensures that the home isn't just a visual delight but also practical for day-to-day living.

Budget, undoubtedly, plays a pivotal role. However, the price tag of a house isn't just the purchase amount. Potential homeowners must factor in additional costs such as property taxes, homeowner's insurance, and potential homeowner association fees. Understanding the complete financial landscape aids in setting a realistic and sustainable budget.

With the digital age upon us, online listings have become a primary tool for home seekers. Websites and apps offer virtual tours, neighborhood statistics, and even insights into future area developments. Yet, while these tools are invaluable, nothing replaces the tactile experience of physically visiting properties. Walking through a space, one can gauge intangible qualities like ambiance, noise levels, and the play of light during different times of the day.

Location, as the age-old real estate adage goes, is every-thing. Beyond just the house itself, the surrounding community, available amenities, public transport links, and future infrastructure projects can significantly influence both the living experience and the property's future appreciation.

It's prudent to remember that the home-buying process can be a marathon, not a sprint. There might be instances of missed opportunities or properties that don't quite align with expectations. Patience and persistence are crucial. Each viewing, negotiation, and consideration is a learning experience, refining one's understanding of what they truly seek in a home.

Lastly, as one navigates this journey, it's beneficial to remain open-minded. While a wishlist is essential, sometimes a property might offer an unexpected charm or potential that wasn't initially on the radar. Being open to possibilities and occasionally recalibrating expectations can lead to delightful discoveries.

Establishing Clear Criteria

A well-defined set of criteria will make your home search more efficient and prevent you from getting sidetracked by properties that aren't truly aligned with your needs and desires.

Location: Understand the neighborhoods that suit your lifestyle and preferences. Consider proximity to work, schools, transportation, shopping, dining, and recreational facilities.

Size and Layout: Determine the number of bedrooms and bathrooms you need. Do you want an open floor plan? Does a home office or a finished basement rank high on your wishlist?

Age and Condition: Are you looking for a new build, a historic property, or something in between? Decide if you're open to taking on a fixer-upper or if you want a move-in ready home.

Amenities: List out the amenities you desire, such as a pool, a large garden, a garage, energy-efficient appliances, or smart home features.

Price Range: Stick to homes within your budget. This will prevent the heartbreak of falling in love with a property you can't afford.

Making the Most of Property Viewings

You're likely to tour multiple properties, so it's crucial to maximize each visit.

Schedule Wisely: Weekend open houses can be crowded. If possible, consider viewing homes on weekdays to have more one-on-one time with the listing agent and to explore the property at your own pace.

Take Notes and Photos: After seeing numerous homes, they might start to blur together. Jot down what you liked and disliked about each property. Take photos to refresh your memory later, but always ask for permission first.

Pay Attention to Red Flags: While cosmetic issues can be easily fixed, structural problems or issues like mold, old roofing, or a cracked foundation can be expensive to address.

Envision Your Life: Think about your daily routines and how they would fit into the space. Would your furniture fit? Is there enough storage? How's the natural light in the main living areas?

Ask Questions: This is where your agent can be an invaluable resource. They can provide insights into things like property taxes, utility costs, and any homeowner association (HOA) fees.

Staying Open-minded

While it's essential to have a clear vision of what you want, being too rigid can prolong your search or cause you to miss out on great properties.

Prioritize: Decide what features you absolutely need versus those you'd like but could live without.

Revisit Your Criteria: After viewing several homes, reflect on your initial criteria. You might discover some aspects are more or less important than you originally thought.

Expand Your Search Area: If you're not finding what you want in your preferred neighborhood, consider expanding your search to nearby areas.

Be Patient, But Decisive: It might take time to find the perfect home, but when you do, be ready to act. In competitive markets, waiting too long can mean missing out on your dream property.

Searching for a home is more than just a sequence of viewings; it's an emotional journey filled with excitement, anticipation, and even occasional setbacks. With a methodical approach, an open mind, and your trusted real estate agent's insights, you're well-equipped to find the perfect place to call home. In our next chapter, we'll discuss making an offer and navigating the complexities of closing the deal.

Chapter 8

Location, Location, Location

The location of a property is one of the most important factors to consider when buying a home. The right location can provide you with access to quality schools, amenities, and transportation, while the wrong location can lead to problems such as noise pollution, traffic congestion, and crime. That's why the phrase "Location, Location, Location" has become synonymous with real estate for good reason. The significance of a property's location transcends its geographical coordinates; it encapsulates the essence of a home's value, its potential for appreciation, and, most importantly, the quality of life it offers its inhabitants.

Researching Neighborhoods and Communities

Before settling on a location, it's prudent to embark on comprehensive research about potential neighborhoods and communities. Websites, local newspapers, and community forums can offer a wealth of information. Attending local community meetings or events can also provide unique insights into the area's ambiance and the cohesiveness of its residents.

The history of a neighborhood can tell tales of its development, transformations, and potential future trajectory. Has it transformed from an industrial hub to a residential haven? Are there plans for future commercial establishments that could influence noise levels or traffic? Such factors can significantly impact daily life and property values.

Factors to Consider: Schools, Amenities, and Transportation

For families, proximity to quality educational institutions is paramount. The reputation and performance of local schools can not only influence a child's education but also affect the property's desirability and resale value.

Amenities, too, play a crucial role. The presence of parks, recreational facilities, shopping centers, and healthcare institutions can elevate the quality of life. For some, a vibrant nightlife or cultural scene might be desirable, while others might prioritize tranquility and green spaces.

Transportation links are pivotal, especially in urban areas. Proximity to public transit options, major highways, and the average commute time to work or essential services can influence daily routines and overall satisfaction with a location.

Future Developments

While a location might seem perfect in the present, it's essential to gauge its future potential. Are there plans for infrastructure projects, like highways or transit lines, that could influence noise levels or property values? Is the area poised for significant commercial or residential development that could alter its character?

The Intangible Essence of a Location

Beyond the tangible attributes, locations carry an intangible essence— a vibe, if you will. Some areas emanate a youthful, dynamic energy, while others exude a serene, laid-back ambiance. This essence, often shaped by its history, residents, and cultural influences, contributes significantly to the living experience. It's something that can't always be quantified but can be felt when walking the streets, interacting with residents, or experiencing its day-to-day rhythm.

When it comes to real estate, the significance of "Location, Location, Location" can't be overstated. It's a multifaceted consideration that influences not just the value of a property but also the very fabric of daily life. By delving deep into the various facets of a location, homebuyers can make informed decisions, ensuring their new home aligns with both their practical needs and lifestyle aspirations.

Here are some of the factors to consider when choosing a location for your home:

- **Schools and education:** The quality of nearby schools is important for families with children. Research school ratings, test scores, and available programs to find the best schools for your family.

- **Proximity to amenities:** Check for nearby shopping centers, grocery stores, and restaurants. Think about the variety and quality of options available.

- **Recreation and green spaces:** Parks, hiking trails, and recreational centers can enhance quality of life and boost property values.

- **Healthcare:** The accessibility of hospitals, clinics, and other healthcare providers can be crucial, especially for older adults or those with ongoing medical needs.

- **Cultural attractions:** Consider theaters, museums, libraries, and other cultural hubs that can enrich community life.

- **Transportation and commute:** If applicable, research the efficiency, coverage, and cost of public transit systems. Proximity to bus stops, train stations, or other transit points can be vital for non-drivers.

- **Highways and main roads:** Easy access to main roads and highways can reduce commute times and provide better access to amenities.

- **Traffic patterns:** While being close to major roads can be a boon, it might also bring noise and congestion. Gauge traffic patterns during different times of the day.

- **Walkability and bike paths:** Some prefer neighborhoods where most essential amenities are within walking or biking distance.

Research the safety and availability of pedestrian paths.

- **Planned infrastructure:** Upcoming infrastructure projects, like new roads or transit lines, can significantly impact property values, either positively or negatively.

- **New developments:** Find out about any planned housing or commercial developments. While they can bring in amenities, they might also alter the character of the neighborhood or increase congestion.

- **Environmental concerns:** Are there any future projects that might affect the local environment? This could include things like landfills, power plants, or large-scale farming operations.

By thoroughly researching schools, amenities, transportation, and potential future developments, you'll be well-equipped to choose a location that not only meets your immediate needs but also promises growth, comfort, and happiness for years to come.

Chapter 9

Making an Offer and Negotiating

After extensive research, property viewings, and considering various neighborhoods, you've finally found the home that feels right. Now comes one of the most critical phases of the home-buying process: making an offer and navigating the negotiations. While emotions can run high during this period, understanding the mechanics of this phase and approaching it with a strategic mindset can make all the difference.

Making an offer and negotiating are critical junctures in the home-buying journey, where dreams meet reality, aspirations align with financial capacities, and a potential buyer takes definitive steps toward home-ownership. While the quest to find the perfect home is indeed a blend of excitement, emotion, and exploration, making an offer grounds this quest in the pragmatic world of numbers, legalities, and strategic decision-making.

The act of making an offer is a declaration of serious intent. It communicates to the seller that you're not just interested, but you're committed enough to take formal action. However, this step, laden with significance, isn't just about stating a price. It encapsulates a myriad of factors — from under-standing the property's true value and anticipating potential competition to assessing one's own finan-cial health and readiness.

Following the offer is the phase of negotiation, an art as much as it is a skill. Negotiating isn't just about getting the best price; it's about crafting an agree-ment that's fair, sustainable, and in alignment with both the buyer's and seller's objectives. This dance of give-and-take requires a keen understanding of mar-ket dynamics, an ability to read and respond to the parties involved, and, importantly, the clarity to differentiate between one's 'wants' and 'needs.'

The process of making an offer and negotiating isn't siloed; it's deeply interconnected with other stages of the home-buying process. It can be influenced by the findings of a home inspection, the outcomes of mortgage pre-approval, or the expertise of a real estate agent guiding the buyer. Navigating these waters requires a blend of preparation, understanding, and strategy, all while keeping emotions in check.

By delving deeper into the intricacies of making an offer and the nuances of negotiation, potential home-buyers arm themselves with the knowledge and insights required to make informed decisions. Decisions that will lay the foundation for what is often one of life's most significant investments. This journey, while potentially daunting, is a rite of passage into home-ownership, and understanding its facets can transform it from a challenge into an empowering experience.

How to Determine an Offer Price

Comparative Market Analysis (CMA): Your real estate agent will often provide a CMA, which compares the prices of recently sold homes that are similar in size, location, and features. This provides a realistic benchmark for determining your offer.

Current Market Conditions: Are you in a buyer's or seller's market? In a seller's market, where demand outpaces supply, homes might sell above the asking price. In a buyer's market, you may have more leverage to negotiate below the asking price.

Home's Time on Market: A home that's been on the market for a considerable period might indicate a seller who's willing to negotiate.

Upcoming Expenses: Consider potential costs like repairs or upgrades. If the house needs significant work, it can be a point of negotiation in the offer price.

Understanding Contingencies

Inspection Contingency: This allows buyers to have the home inspected within a specified period, offering an option to renegotiate or withdraw the offer without penalty if significant issues are uncovered.

Financing Contingency: This protects the buyer in case they're unable to secure a mortgage for the property. If financing falls through and this contingency is in place, the buyer can withdraw from the deal.

Appraisal Contingency: If a home's appraisal value comes in below the offer price, this contingency lets buyers renegotiate or back out. It ensures you don't overpay compared to the lender's valuation of the home.

Home Sale Contingency: Some buyers might need to sell their current home to finance the new purchase. This contingency allows buyers a set period to sell their existing property before proceeding with the purchase.

The Art of Negotiation

Stay Informed: Understand all the factors mentioned above and use them to your advantage. An informed buyer, backed by a knowledgeable agent, stands a better chance in negotiations.

Emotional Detachment: It's essential to approach negotiations from a position of objectivity. Remember, there's always another house, and it's crucial not to overextend or make hasty decisions based on emotions.

Be Ready to Compromise: While it's important to have clear boundaries on what you're willing to spend and which terms you're comfortable with, some level of compromise can smooth out the negotiation process.

Clear Communication: Always ensure open channels of communication, primarily through your agent. Misunderstandings or delays can sour a potential deal.

Multiple Offers: In hot markets, be prepared for bidding wars. Decide your upper limit and stick to it to avoid being caught in the heat of the moment.

Making an offer and navigating the subsequent negotiations is a delicate balance of strategy, patience, and
sometimes, swift decision-making. By understanding
the nuances of determining an offer price, being clear
about contingencies, and mastering the art of negotiation, you'll be well-positioned to secure the home of
your dreams on terms that work for you. In the chapters ahead, we'll delve deeper into the closing process
and ensuring a smooth transition to your new home.

Chapter 10

Home Inspections and Appraisals

Once you've negotiated an offer and entered into a purchase agreement, the home-buying process moves into a phase of verification and validation. At this stage, home inspections and appraisals take center stage. Both of these evaluations are crucial, ensuring that you're making a sound investment. While they may seem like additional hurdles, they offer protection and clarity for the buyer. Embarking on this stage of the journey beckons a shift from the emotional exhilaration of finding a potential home to the analytical rigor of ensuring its worthiness.

A home inspection, at its core, is like a comprehensive health check-up for the property. It dives beneath the aesthetic allure, seeking out hidden flaws, underlying issues, or potential future complications. This process isn't about nitpicking every minor flaw but about obtaining a clear-eyed view of the property's condition. The revelations from an inspection can influence negotiations, inform repair decisions, and in some cases, even prompt a reconsideration of the purchase.

On the other side of the coin, we have appraisals — an endeavor to pinpoint the home's monetary worth in the current market landscape. While buyers and sellers may have their subjective valuations, appraisals bring in an objective lens, grounded in market trends, comparable sales, and the property's unique features. This ensures that buyers are neither overextending themselves financially nor undervaluing a potential gem. The appraisal is typically done by the lender to ensure the property they are extending credit for you to purchase is actually worth what they are lending.

Yet, it's essential to understand that both inspections and appraisals aren't merely transactional processes. They're protective layers, safeguarding a buyer from unforeseen costs, and ensuring that the significant financial investment aligns with the property's actual value. Beyond their tangible benefits, these processes also provide peace of mind, solidifying a buyer's confidence in their decision.

As we delve deeper into this chapter, we'll unravel the intricacies and nuances of home inspections and appraisals. Through understanding their significance, prospective homeowners are better equipped to navigate these stages with informed discernment, ensuring that their journey to homeownership is both joyful and judicious.

The Importance of a Thorough Home Inspection

Risk Mitigation: A home inspection is a comprehensive review of the property's physical condition. It identifies potential issues, from minor cosmetic flaws to major structural problems, giving buyers a clearer understanding of what they're committing to.

Financial Planning: By uncovering necessary repairs or replacements, an inspection helps buyers anticipate additional costs. This can inform decisions on a suitable emergency fund or maintenance budget.

Long-term Security: Beyond immediate issues, a home inspection can shed light on the longevity of key components, like the roof or HVAC system. This aids in future planning.

Negotiation Power: If significant problems are detected, buyers can use the inspection report as a tool to renegotiate terms, ask for repairs, or even adjust the purchase price.

What Happens During an Appraisal

Objective Property Valuation: An appraisal provides an unbiased estimate of the home's value. Conducted by a licensed appraiser, this process takes into account recent sales of similar properties, the home's condition, size, location, and other influential factors.

Lender Requirements: Lenders mandate appraisals to ensure the amount they're loaning aligns with the property's true value. If an appraisal comes in below the agreed purchase price, lenders might offer a smaller loan amount, reflecting the appraised value.

Buyer Assurance: Beyond lender requirements, an appraisal can provide peace of mind. It reaffirms that the buyer isn't overpaying for the property.

Addressing Issues and Renegotiating

Reviewing Inspection Results: Once you receive the inspection report, review it carefully with your agent. Identify any significant concerns and decide what you're willing to handle versus what you'd like the seller to address.

Renegotiation Strategies

Price Reduction: If there are considerable repairs or updates required, buyers can ask for a decrease in the purchase price.

Seller Repairs: Instead of a price adjustment, buyers can request that the seller make necessary repairs before closing.

Escrow Funds: Another option is for the seller to deposit funds into escrow, which will cover specific repair costs after closing.

Appraisal Shortfalls: If the appraisal value is below the purchase price, buyers can:

Negotiate a Lower Price: Approach the seller to adjust the price in line with the appraisal.

Challenge the Appraisal: If there are discrepancies or overlooked comparable sales, you can request a review or order a second appraisal.

Increase Down Payment: If renegotiation isn't feasible, buyers can make up the difference between the loan amount and purchase price out of pocket.

Home inspections and appraisals are pivotal components of the home-buying journey, safeguarding buyers from potential pitfalls and ensuring a fair transaction. By understanding their importance and being
prepared to address any issues they uncover, you're
one step closer to a successful home purchase. In the
subsequent chapters, we'll explore the closing process
and the final steps to claiming your new home.

Chapter 11

When Deals Go Wrong

The intricate world of real estate is a blend of excitement, anticipation, and, at times, unexpected hurdles. While every homebuyer and seller wishes for a smooth transition from the initial agreement to the closing handshake, the road is occasionally punctuated with challenges that can derail even the most promising of deals.

One of the primary culprits behind faltering deals is financial hiccups. Picture this: a buyer has secured a mortgage pre-approval, but upon deeper scrutiny, this approval gets overturned due to reasons like a sudden change in employment status, a dip in credit scores, or previously undisclosed debts. Additionally, there are moments when a home's appraised value falls short of its selling price. This gap can strain the buyer's finances, potentially causing the deal to unravel unless both parties can renegotiate terms.

Home inspections, while essential, can sometimes unearth unanticipated issues. Major problems, such as foundational cracks, outdated electrical systems, or deteriorating roofs, can cast shadows of doubt in buyers' minds. The apprehension stemming from these discoveries can lead to either a renegotiation of the property price or, in some cases, the withdrawal of the initial offer altogether.

The paperwork accompanying a property sale isn't immune to complications either. Title disputes, often arising from undisclosed heirs, existing liens, or other legal entanglements, can stall or even nullify a deal. A clear title is a non-negotiable element of real estate transactions, and any ambiguity can be a deal-breaker.

On the emotional front, buyer's remorse can be a significant factor. The realization of the sheer scale of the purchase, coupled with the long-term commitment, can lead some buyers to rethink their decisions. This emotional recalibration can, at times, result in the termination of the agreement. Additionally, contingency clauses, such as the sale of the buyer's existing home, can introduce variables that, if unfulfilled, can dissolve the deal.

Misaligned timelines between buyer and seller often pose challenges as well. If a buyer is in a hurry to relocate but the seller encounters delays in vacating the property, it can introduce tension and potential cancellations. Moreover, external economic shifts, including sudden downturns or interest rate hikes, can transform an affordable loan into an untenable commitment overnight.

However, amidst these challenges lies the silver lining of preparedness. With open communication, a buffer for unexpected hitches, and the guidance of qualified professionals, many of these pitfalls can be navigated successfully. Knowledge, as they say, is power, and in understanding these potential deal-breakers, both buyers and sellers can stride forward with confidence and clarity.

Common Transaction Killers

Financial Hiccups:

- Loan Denials: Even with a pre-approval, a mortgage can be denied upon further inspection. Factors like a change in the buyer's credit score, employment status, or undisclosed debts can tip the scales.

 - Low Appraisals: When a home is appraised below the selling price, it can cause financing issues unless the buyer is willing to cover the difference or the seller is willing to reduce the price.

Home Inspection Surprises:

 An inspection might reveal significant problems, such as structural issues, old roofing, or faulty wiring. Such findings can either scare off buyers or lead to renegotiations, which might not always be successful.

Title Issues:

Before a property can change hands, it needs a clear title. Existing liens, disputes, or undisclosed heirs can halt a deal in its tracks.

Buyer's Remorse:

It's not uncommon for buyers to get cold feet, especially when confronted with the magnitude of the purchase. This emotional response can sometimes lead to a deal's undoing.

Seller's Remorse:

Yup, they get it too sometimes!

Contingency Clauses:

Many contracts include contingencies, like the sale of the buyer's existing home. If these conditions aren't met, the deal can dissolve.

Mismatched Timelines:

Buyers and sellers can sometimes have differing timelines. If a buyer needs to move in before the seller is ready to vacate, or if there are delays in the seller's next property purchase, it can cause friction and deal dissolution.

Negotiation Breakdowns:

Post-inspection, buyers might ask for repairs or price reductions. If both parties can't reach an agreement, the deal can fall apart.

External Economic Factors:

Sudden economic downturns, spikes in interest rates, or shifts in the housing market can make previously approved loans unaffordable or unattractive for buyers.

Navigating the Minefield:

While these pitfalls can seem daunting, being forewarned is forearmed. Here are some strategies to navigate them:

- **Build a Buffer:** Always factor in extra time and a financial buffer for unexpected costs or delays.

- **Open Communication:** Regular check-ins with all parties involved – be it your realtor, lender, or the sellers – can preempt many issues.

- **Qualified Professionals:** Ensure you're working with experienced and recommended professionals, from realtors to home inspectors.

In the end, while the journey to home ownership can be riddled with challenges, understanding these potential hiccups prepares you for the journey ahead, making the path to your dream home a bit clearer.

Chapter 12

Understanding and Navigating the Closing Process

Congratulations, you're nearing the final stages of your home-buying journey. The closing process, often viewed as the final lap in the marathon of home-buying, is a tapestry of intricate details, legal formalities, and financial commitments converging to mark the culmination of a buyer's journey. However, to deem it merely as a concluding act would be to oversimplify its importance. This phase isn't just the endgame; it's the crucial moment where aspirations crystallize into reality, where signed documents and exchanged keys transform a property listing into a personal haven.

At the heart of this process lies a complex interplay of multiple stakeholders, from real estate agents, lenders, and title companies to insurers, appraisers, and, of course, the buyer and seller. Each plays a distinct role, ensuring that the myriad legal and financial intricacies are addressed with precision and transparency. The gravity of the closing process is palpable, for it signifies a point of no return — once completed, the deal is sealed, and the journey of homeownership truly commences.

But the path to closing isn't without its challenges. It demands an understanding of closing costs, an anticipation of potential hurdles, and a meticulous review of the contractual obligations. The stakes are high, both in terms of financial outlays and the emotional investment leading up to this moment. As a result, knowledge becomes the prospective homeowner's most potent ally, transforming what could be an

overwhelming whirlwind of paperwork and proce-
dures into a navigable, comprehensible process.

In this chapter, we'll embark on a deep dive into the
closing process's very marrow. We will demystify the
jargon, unpack the sequence of events, and illuminate
the potential pitfalls and how to sidestep them. Our
goal is not just to elucidate the mechanics of closing
but to instill a sense of confidence and empowerment
in every reader, ensuring that when they arrive at the
closing table, they do so with clarity, preparedness,
and the exhilarating anticipation of the new chapter
awaiting them.

Breaking Down Closing Costs

Lender Fees: These are costs related to the processing
and underwriting of your loan. They can include application fees, credit report fees, origination fees, and
more.

Title Services: Title search fees cover the cost of
examining public records to ensure no one else has

a claim to the property. Title insurance, meanwhile, protects the lender (and optionally, the buyer) against any undiscovered claims that might arise in the future.

Prepaid Costs: These are upfront costs for items like property taxes, homeowner's insurance, and possibly homeowner's association fees. They're called "prepaid" because you're paying them in advance of their due date.

Escrow Funds: Your lender might require you to deposit funds into an escrow account to cover future property taxes and insurance premiums.

Appraisal and Inspection Fees: Though you may have already paid these, they're technically considered part of closing costs.

Other Miscellaneous Fees: These can range from notary fees, attorney fees (if applicable in your state or if you chose to have representation), courier fees, and government recording fees.

What to Expect on Closing Day

Final Walk-through: Typically, before the closing meeting, you'll do a final walk-through of the property. This ensures that the home is in the agreed-upon condition and that any required repairs have been made.

Review and Sign Documents: At the closing, you'll be presented with numerous documents, including the deed of trust or mortgage contract, promissory note, and the closing disclosure. Ensure you understand each one and don't hesitate to ask questions. Depending on where you live and the customs on that area, you may or may not do closing formally at a closing table. The west coast of the United States typically handles closings in escrow, where documents are signed a few days before closing. In this scenario the closing day is very informal and there is typically nothing for the buyer to do that day except collect the keys once word is received that the transaction is officially closed.

Payment: You'll need to bring a cashier's check or arrange a wire transfer for your down payment and closing costs.

Receive Keys: Once everything is signed, and funds are distributed, you'll officially receive the keys to your new home!

Common Delays and How to Address Them

Financing Issues: Sometimes, last-minute issues can arise with your mortgage approval. Ensure that you've provided all necessary documentation to your lender and avoid making significant financial changes during the closing process.

Appraisal Discrepancies: If the home appraises for less than the purchase price, it can delay closing unless the price is renegotiated, or the buyer chooses to make up the difference.

Title Issues: Unexpected claims, liens, or disputes can arise. The title company will work to resolve these, but it can introduce delays.

Home Inspection Surprises: Late discoveries about the property's condition might necessitate renegotiations or further repairs.

Buyer or Seller Changes: Either party might request last-minute changes to the agreement, causing potential delays.

The closing process is the final hurdle in your home-buying journey. While it can be nerve-wracking, a clear understanding of the costs involved, knowing what to expect on the day, and being prepared for potential delays can make the experience significantly smoother. As you move on from here, you'll step into your new role as a homeowner, ready to make memories and build a life in your new abode. In the chapters that follow, we'll offer insights into settling into your new home, maintenance tips, and making your house truly yours.

Chapter 13

Special Considerations

Navigating the vast seascape of real estate can sometimes feel like charting unfamiliar waters. The industry, rich in its variety and depth, presents avenues that appeal to different aspirations, be it securing a dream family home, diving into the world of property investments, or seeking out unique buying opportunities like foreclosures. However, just as each opportunity holds the potential for great reward, they also come with their set of intricacies and potential pitfalls.

Foreclosures, for instance, might present an appealing price tag, but understanding the history, condition, and any potential legal complications tied to such properties is essential. Investment properties, while promising lucrative returns in the right market conditions, demand a keen understanding of market trends, tenant rights, and property maintenance. On the other hand, properties within a Homeowners' Association (HOA) community might offer added amenities and a sense of communal living, yet they also come with their specific rules, regulations, and often, additional fees.

This chapter endeavors to be your compass in these varied terrains. Our goal is to shed light on the characteristics, advantages, and challenges of each of these real estate facets. By diving deep into the specifics of foreclosures, investment properties, and HOA-governed homes, we aim to equip you with a holistic understanding. This knowledge will serve as a powerful tool, ensuring you're not just captivated by the allure of potential benefits but are also acutely aware of any associated challenges.

By the end of this chapter, you'll have a clearer vision of these distinct real estate paths, enabling you to weigh pros and cons, assess risks, and confidently stride forward, making decisions that align with your financial goals and personal aspirations. Let's set sail together into these captivating domains of the real estate world, exploring, understanding, and preparing for the journey ahead.

Buying a Foreclosure or Short-sale Property

- **Foreclosure:** When a homeowner fails to meet their mortgage obligations, the lender can seize and sell the property. Foreclosed homes are often auctioned or sold by the bank.

- **Short-sale:** This is when a homeowner sells their property for less than the outstanding mortgage balance, usually with lender approval, as an alternative to foreclosure.

Advantages:

*- **Potential for Lower Prices:** Foreclosed and short-sale properties can often be purchased below market value.

*- **Opportunity for Investment:** With the right improvements, these properties can offer substantial ROI.

Challenges:

*- **Condition of the Property:** Foreclosed properties may have been vacant for a while and could have maintenance issues. Short-sales, meanwhile, might have been neglected due to the owner's financial struggles.

*- **Complex Purchase Process:** The buying process, especially for short-sales, can be lengthier and requires more paperwork.

Tips for Success:

*- **Do Thorough Research:** Understand the local market, the history of the property, and any associated liabilities.

- Get a Home Inspection: This is crucial to identify potential issues and assess the cost of repairs.

Investing in Real Estate: What's Different

Mindset Shift: Investing in real estate is different from buying a primary residence. The focus is less on personal preferences and more on profitability and market trends.

Research is Key: Understand local rental markets, property appreciation trends, and tenant demographics.

Cost Considerations: Beyond the purchase price, consider property taxes, maintenance costs, management fees (if you hire a property manager), and potential vacancy periods.

Financing Differences: Mortgage terms and rates can differ for investment properties, often requiring larger down payments.

Rental Management: Decide if you'll manage the property yourself or hire a professional. Each has its own set of challenges and costs.

Buying Properties in HOA Communities: Pros and Cons

What's an HOA?: Homeowners' Associations are organizations that create and enforce rules within a community. Property owners pay fees to the HOA, which are used for community maintenance and amenities.

Advantages:

- **Uniform Standards:** HOAs maintain aesthetic and structural standards, which can uphold property values.

- **Amenities:** Many HOA communities offer shared amenities like pools, gyms, and parks.

- **Dispute Mediation:** HOAs can handle disputes between neighbors, such as property line issues or noise complaints.

Drawbacks:

- **Fees:** HOA dues can be expensive and might increase over time.

- **Restrictions:** HOAs often have stringent rules about property modifications, pet ownership, and more.

- **Potential for Conflict:** Disagreements between homeowners and HOA boards can arise over rule enforcement or financial matters.

Navigating these special considerations in the real estate world requires a blend of research, expert guidance, and a clear understanding of your goals. Whether you're looking for a bargain, an investment, or a community with specific amenities, understanding the nuances of each scenario will position you for success. As we journey forward, we'll continue to explore more unique facets of the real estate world, equipping you for any venture you choose to embark upon.

Chapter 14

The Allure of Green Homes: Eco-friendly Real Estate

I n an era where environmental concerns rank high on global agendas, the rise of green homes has been nothing short of revolutionary. These eco-friendly abodes, while promising a sustainable lifestyle, also come with their own set of considerations and nuances in the real estate market. For those considering stepping into this vibrant realm of green housing, understanding the intricacies can make the journey smoother and more rewarding.

The rise of green homes is a testament to a modern age where sustainable living is not just a choice, but often a pressing need. This evolution wasn't merely about constructing houses with recycled materials; it signaled a more profound societal realization. It reflected our growing recognition of the Earth's fragility and a shared responsibility to reduce our environmental impact.

These eco-friendly homes, dubbed 'green' not just for their minimized environmental footprint but also for pioneering fresh standards, represent an intersection of architectural innovation and ecological stewardship. From harnessing solar energy to promoting water conservation and utilizing locally sourced, sustainable building materials, these homes are holistic in their green approach. They don't just exist in isolation; they interact, adapt, and contribute positively to their environments.

However, with innovation comes complexity. The green housing sector, while transformative, also introduces layers of intricacies that are distinct from the traditional real estate market. For instance, the materials and technologies used in green homes might be unfamiliar to many. Understanding the efficiency of a photovoltaic solar panel system, or the benefits of rammed earth walls, requires a different knowledge base than that of conventional homes.

Additionally, the valuation of green homes might not always align with standard market rates. Their worth is encapsulated not just in square footage or location, but also in the promise of reduced utility bills, the longevity of sustainable materials, and sometimes, the social currency of living sustainably.

For prospective homeowners or investors looking to delve into this burgeoning segment of the market, the green home journey can appear daunting. Yet, with the right information, guidance, and perspective, navigating this realm can be immensely fulfilling. Beyond acquiring a piece of real estate, it's about investing in a sustainable future, aligning personal values with living choices, and becoming part of a global movement towards a more harmonious coexistence with our planet.

The Green Difference

At the core of a green home is its commitment to sustainability, energy efficiency, and a reduced carbon footprint. These houses often incorporate innovative technologies, natural materials, and designs that prioritize both the environment and inhabitants' well-being. While this might sound idyllic, the transactions involving such properties can differ from conventional real estate deals.

Specialized Assessments: Green homes often require specialized home inspectors familiar with eco-friendly technologies and materials. Traditional home assessments might overlook or misinterpret some of the unique features and systems in a green home.

Valuation Variances: Green homes can sometimes have a higher upfront cost, reflecting the investment in sustainable technologies. However, the long-term savings in energy costs can balance out the initial expenditure. It's crucial to approach appraisals with a broader perspective, considering both the immediate price tag and long-term financial implications.

Financing and Incentives: Some financial institutions offer specialized loans or incentives for eco-friendly home purchases, recognizing the value of sustainable investments. Researching and tapping into these can yield financial benefits.

Considerations for Green Home Buyers

For potential buyers drawn to the allure of green homes, certain factors can inform and elevate their purchase journey.

Authenticity Check: 'Greenwashing', a term used when properties are falsely marketed as eco-friendly, is an emerging concern. Buyers should verify claims by checking for certifications like LEED (Leadership in Energy and Environmental Design) or other recognized environmental benchmarks.

Understanding the Tech: Green homes often feature advanced systems like solar panels, geothermal heating, or gray water recycling. Familiarizing oneself with these technologies, their maintenance, and their benefits can lead to informed decisions.

Future-Proofing: Eco-friendly homes are designed for the future. But as technology and sustainability practices evolve, ensuring that the home can adapt to newer advancements is key. For instance, homes with modular designs might be more adaptable to future green upgrades.

Holistic Neighborhood Assessment: A green home's environment can amplify its benefits. Prioritizing neighborhoods that support eco-friendly living, such as those with efficient public transport, community gardens, or shared recycling programs, can enhance the green living experience.

Resale Value: While the green home market is burgeoning, it's still nascent compared to conventional real estate. Buyers should consider the potential resale value, keeping in mind that as environmental awareness grows, the demand for green homes is likely to rise.

Embracing the ethos of a green home is more than a mere real estate acquisition; it's a profound commitment to a sustainable ethos that reverberates through time. This journey, while rooted in the present desire to reduce one's carbon footprint, extends its branches into the future, painting a vision of harmonious living for generations to come.

When one chooses to invest in a green home, they're not just purchasing walls, floors, and roofs. They're investing in a legacy—a pledge to future generations that underscores a dedication to preserving the world they inherit. This is a tangible manifestation of an individual's dedication to combating the global environmental crises we face. The house becomes a living, breathing testament to a way of life that prioritizes the planet's health and well-being.

But the path to realizing this vision, like all transformative journeys, is layered with complexities and considerations. Aligning personal choices with broader environmental imperatives means more than just understanding the specifics of green technologies and materials. It's about integrating an ecological perspective into daily routines, making conscious decisions that resonate with this overarching objective of sustainability.

Knowledge becomes the bedrock of this endeavor. Being well-informed about the intricacies of green homes, from their construction nuances to their long-term benefits, paves the way for informed choices. Research, a tool often underestimated, illuminates the path, offering insights into evolving technologies, sustainable practices, and emerging trends. Foresight, the ability to envision the long-term implications of today's decisions, ensures that the choices made today remain relevant, effective, and beneficial in the decades to come.

Thus, as one stands on the precipice of this green journey, it's essential to recognize that the steps taken are laden with significance. With the right blend of information, vision, and commitment, the dream of sustainable living becomes more than just an aspiration. It evolves into a deeply gratifying reality, where every corner of the home whispers tales of responsibility, innovation, and hope for a brighter, greener future.

Chapter 15

Moving In and Beyond

The closing is complete, and the keys are in your hand—your new home awaits. While the buying process was a journey of its own, transitioning into your new space and ensuring its long-term value also requires effort and foresight. This chapter provides guidelines for a seamless move, tips for settling in, and strategies to protect and enhance your property's worth.

Transitioning into a new space is akin to stitching a new chapter into the tapestry of one's life. It's not just about shifting furniture or unpacking boxes; it's about imprinting your personal ethos onto the very walls and rooms, transforming a structure of brick and mortar into a sanctuary echoing with warmth, memories, and aspirations. This phase, however, is not without its hurdles. How do you strike a balance between immediate comfort and long-term functionality? What choices and arrangements will ease your daily routines, reflecting not just your present needs but also accommodating your future endeavors?

Beyond the immediacy of moving in and settling down, there lies the expansive horizon of maintaining your home. This isn't merely about regular upkeep or occasional renovations. It's a strategic dance of decisions that not only preserve but also enhance the value of your property. As markets evolve and neighborhoods change, being attuned to these dynamics can ensure that your investment, both emotional and financial, continues to reap dividends.

Dive in, for the journey of "home" has only just begun.

Preparing for the Move: A Checklist

Hire a Reputable Moving Company: Research and gather quotes from several moving companies. Ensure they're licensed and insured, and read reviews from previous customers.

Declutter and Donate: Before packing, go through your belongings and decide what you truly need. Donate, sell, or dispose of items you no longer use.

Pack Smart: Label boxes clearly by room and contents. Consider what items you'll need immediately and pack those separately.

Notify Important Parties: Inform your bank, credit card companies, post office, utility providers, and other essential contacts about your address change.

Prepare a Moving Day Kit: This should include essentials like toiletries, a change of clothes, important documents, medications, snacks, and anything else you might need before unpacking.

Settling In: Post-purchase Essentials

Safety First: Change all locks and ensure windows have working locks. Test smoke alarms and carbon monoxide detectors, and locate the main water shut-off valve.

Utilities and Services: Ensure all utilities are switched to your name and set up any needed services like trash collection or internet.

Familiarize Yourself with the Home: Locate the electrical panel, the main water valve, and other essential areas of your home. Understanding your home's systems will help in emergencies and routine maintenance.

Introduce Yourself to Neighbors: Building a rapport with neighbors not only fosters a sense of community but can also be advantageous for security and local advice.

Maintaining and Increasing Your Home's Value

Routine Maintenance: Regularly inspect your home for signs of wear and tear. Cleaning gutters, changing air filters, and checking for leaks can prevent more significant, costly issues down the line.

Invest in Quality Improvements: Renovations should be both aesthetically pleasing and functional. Prioritize upgrades that offer good returns on investment, such as kitchen and bathroom remodels.

Landscaping and Curb Appeal: The exterior of your home is the first impression it gives. Regularly mow the lawn, trim hedges, and invest in some attractive plants or flowers.

Stay Informed about the Market: Even if you're not planning to sell soon, keeping an eye on local real estate trends will give you an idea of your property's value and potential areas of improvement.

Energy Efficiency: Modern buyers value energy-efficient homes. Consider upgrades like double-paned windows, insulation, or solar panels, which can both reduce your utility bills and boost your home's value.

As you settle into your new space, the focus shifts from purchasing to preservation and enhancement. By attentively preparing for your move, ensuring a comfortable and safe transition, and maintaining your home with an eye towards its long-term value, you lay the foundation for countless memories and potential future gains. In the chapters ahead, we'll delve into deeper home improvement strategies, sustainable living, and creating a home that's not only a dwelling but a reflection of your unique personality and values.

Chapter 16

The Responsibilities of Homeownership

Owning a home isn't just about having a place to rest your head—it's about cultivating a space that grows with you, reflects your values, and serves as a foundation for your future. But with this ownership comes a significant responsibility. It's not just about aesthetics; it's about ensuring the house's longevity and safety.

Regular maintenance is crucial. Just like a car needs its oil changed and tires rotated, a home needs consistent care. Simple tasks, like cleaning gutters, inspecting the roof, or servicing the HVAC system, can prevent bigger issues down the road. These tasks might seem minor, but they're the key to avoiding major repairs and keeping your home running smoothly.

Over the years, there are also larger tasks that can't be avoided. Maybe it's repainting the exterior, replacing old windows, or updating outdated plumbing. While these projects might require more investment, they're essential for maintaining your home's value and ensuring its longevity.

And then there's safety—a paramount concern for every homeowner. Whether it's ensuring the house is equipped with functional smoke alarms, setting up a reliable security system, or checking for potential hazards around the property, it's a homeowner's duty to ensure their space is safe and secure.

In this chapter, we'll dive deeper into the intricate dance of home maintenance. We'll discuss not only the how-tos but also the whys, ensuring you're well-prepared to tackle any challenge your home might present, keeping it in top condition for years to come.

Routine Maintenance Checks

There are a few key areas of your home that should be checked regularly for signs of wear and tear. These include:

- **HVAC systems:** Make sure your heating, ventilation, and air conditioning systems are working properly. Change the filters regularly and have them inspected by a professional annually.

- **Roof and gutters:** Inspect your roof for any missing shingles, signs of water damage, or other issues. Clean out your gutters seasonally to prevent blockages that can lead to water damage.

- **Plumbing:** Check for any leaks in faucets, toilets, and under sinks. Address small issues early to prevent costly repairs later.

- **Electrical systems:** Regularly test all outlets and ensure your circuit breaker is functioning correctly. Look out for any signs of faulty wiring, like flickering lights or strange sounds.

Seasonal Tasks

In addition to routine maintenance, there are a few seasonal tasks that should be done to keep your home in good condition. These include:

- Winterizing: Before the cold sets in, insulate any exposed pipes, seal gaps in doors and windows, and ensure your heating system is functioning optimally.

- Spring cleaning: This season is ideal for deep cleaning your home, checking for damage

from winter, and preparing your garden or
yard for the warmer months.

- **Summer:** Check your home's external paint
  for chipping, service your air conditioning
  system, and clean the vents and exhausts.

- **Fall preparations:** Clean out gutters, inspect your home for any cracks that need seal-
  ing, and prepare for winter by ensuring all
  insulation is intact.

Long-term Upkeep

In addition to routine maintenance and seasonal
tasks, there are a few long-term upkeep tasks that will
need to be done to keep your home in good condition.
These include:

- **Pest control:** Periodically inspect your home
  for signs of pests, such as termites, which can
  cause significant damage if unchecked. Consider annual inspections by professionals.

- **Foundation:** Check for any cracks or shifts in your home's foundation. Addressing these early can save significant costs and potential safety issues down the line.

- **Landscaping:** Trees near your home should be pruned to prevent them from causing damage in storms. Also, ensure plants near your home's foundation have adequate drainage to prevent water-related issues.

Safety Considerations

Finally, there are a few safety considerations that should be kept in mind when owning a home. These include:

- **Emergency protocols:** Regularly review and practice your emergency plans, ensuring all family members are aware. Keep emergency kits up to date.

- **Smoke and CO detectors:** Regularly test

and replace the batteries in all detectors. These simple devices can be life-saving.

- **Security systems:** Periodically review the functionality of your security systems, updating as necessary.

By following these tips, you can help ensure that your home is a safe and comfortable place to live for many years to come.

Chapter 17

Enhancing and Remodeling: Increasing Your Home's Value

As the years go by, the ebb and flow of life can lead to evolving desires and preferences. Just as we change our wardrobe to align with shifting fashions or our personal growth, our homes too can benefit from a revamp to reflect our current tastes and needs. Additionally, the dynamic world of home design is always presenting new trends, innovative styles, and cutting-edge functionalities. Some homeowners might feel the itch to remodel out of a desire to stay modern, while others might be thinking of the potential market value their home could fetch should they decide to sell.

Entering the realm of home remodeling is not just about aesthetic alterations—it's about striking the perfect balance between personal gratification and financial prudence. While it's wonderful to have a newly renovated kitchen or a beautifully landscaped garden to enjoy, it's equally crucial to consider the financial implications. Will this remodel add substantial value to your home? Is the cost of remodeling balanced out by the potential increase in your property's worth?

This chapter aims to be your guide through the intricate paths of home remodeling. We'll delve into the world of popular home upgrades, dissecting the ones that not only elevate your living experience but also promise a healthy return on investment. From kitchen makeovers and bathroom upgrades to outdoor additions and energy-efficient improvements, we'll navigate the pros, cons, and expected ROIs.

Whether you're contemplating a significant home overhaul or just a few minor tweaks, this chapter seeks to arm you with the knowledge you need. Let's embark on this remodeling journey, blending personal aspirations with wise investment choices, ensuring your home remains a haven of comfort, style, and value.

Understanding ROI in Home Improvements

What is ROI?: ROI measures the return you can expect from an investment, relative to its cost. In the context of home improvements, it refers to the percentage of the project's cost you're likely to recoup in increased home value.

Prioritizing High-ROI Projects: While some upgrades are primarily for personal enjoyment, if you're making improvements with an eye towards selling, it's wise to prioritize projects known for a high return.

Projects with High ROI

Kitchen Remodel: The kitchen is often considered the heart of the home. Even minor updates can offer a significant return. Consider new countertops, updated appliances, or refaced cabinetry.

Bathroom Updates: Modernizing an old bathroom or adding an additional one can significantly increase a home's value. Think about adding modern fixtures, efficient lighting, or even radiant floor heating.

Enhancing Curb Appeal: First impressions matter. Landscaping, a fresh coat of paint, or a new front door can drastically improve your home's exterior appearance.

Energy-Efficient Upgrades: With increasing awareness of environmental concerns and rising energy costs, homes that boast energy-efficient features can be more appealing. Consider double-paned windows, enhanced attic insulation, or efficient appliances.

Projects for Personal Enjoyment

Home Office: In an increasingly remote-working world, a well-equipped and comfortable home office has become a desirable feature.

Outdoor Living Spaces: Decks, patios, and outdoor kitchens can extend your living space and offer a fresh area to relax and entertain.

Basement or Attic Conversion: Transforming these often-underutilized spaces into livable areas like a game room, guest room, or home gym can add both value and function to your home.

Smart Home Upgrades: Introducing features like smart thermostats, security systems, or automated lighting can add modern convenience to your living space.

Navigating the Remodeling Process

Planning: Define clear objectives for your remodel. Are you looking for increased comfort, functionality, or higher resale value?

- Consider your needs and wants for your home.

- Research different remodeling options and costs.

- Create a budget and timeline for your project.

Budgeting: Set a clear budget, factoring in a buffer for unexpected expenses. It's also wise to consult with local real estate agents or appraisers to understand how your planned improvements might influence your home's value in the local market.

- Get multiple estimates from contractors.

- Be sure to include the cost of materials, labor, and permits in your budget.

- Allow for a contingency fund for unexpected costs.

Hiring Professionals: While some projects are suitable for the DIY approach, others require professional expertise. Research and choose contractors with a proven track record.

- Get references from friends, family, or other homeowners.

- Check online reviews and licensing information.

- Interview multiple contractors before making a decision.

Permits and Regulations: Ensure that any significant remodeling adheres to local building codes and regulations. Acquire necessary permits before beginning work.

- Contact your local building department to find out about the requirements for your project.

- File for the necessary permits and pay any associated fees.

- Follow all building codes and regulations during construction.

Remodeling and enhancing your home can be a rewarding endeavor, both emotionally and financially. Whether you're looking to stay in your home for years to come or considering selling in the foreseeable future, informed decisions will ensure you maximize both your enjoyment and your investment. In the next chapter, we'll explore the intricacies of selling your home, ensuring a smooth and profitable transition to your next adventure.

Here are some final tips for remodeling your home:

- Be realistic about your budget and timeline.

- Don't be afraid to ask for help from professionals.

- Be patient and enjoy the process!

Chapter 18

Embracing Homeownership: Next Steps and Future Considerations

Owning a home is more than just a checkmark on the list of life's accomplishments—it represents stability, achievement, and personal space. It's where memories are made, families grow, and life stories unfold. While the allure of homeownership lies partly in the allure of achieving a widely-held aspiration, it's also deeply intertwined with the nuanced experiences, both highs and lows, that come with it.

Throughout this guide, we've delved into the intricate steps leading up to that precious moment when you hold the keys to your new abode. From understanding your finances to navigating negotiations, and from inspections to the actual move-in, you've been equipped with a comprehensive toolkit to make informed decisions. But owning a home isn't just about the initial purchase—it's an evolving journey.

This journey involves late nights fixing that unexpected leak, the joy of personalizing each nook and cranny to reflect your tastes, the satisfaction of a well-maintained garden, or the community of neighbors that becomes an extended family. And as time goes on, you may find yourself considering renovations, upgrades, or even a future move, further adding layers to your homeownership narrative.

As we wrap up this guide, our aim is not to signal the end but to emphasize the beginning of your unique homeownership story. This conclusion is an invitation to embrace every facet of owning a home—the challenges that test your patience, the milestones worth celebrating, and the countless everyday moments in between. So, with a foundation of knowledge and an eye toward the future, step confidently into the next chapters of your homeownership journey, cherishing every twist and turn along the way.

Embracing the New Chapter

Continual Learning: Homeownership, with its multitude of facets, is an ongoing education. Stay abreast of new home trends, maintenance best practices, and market shifts. As seasons change and years pass, your home and its needs will evolve.

Building Community: One of the greatest joys of settling in a new place is forging connections. Engage with your neighbors, participate in local events, and contribute to making your community vibrant and supportive.

Personalizing Your Space: A house becomes a home when it's imbued with personal touches. Infuse your personality into each room, and don't be afraid to reinvent spaces as your tastes change.

Future Considerations

Refinancing: As economic landscapes and personal finances shift, you might consider refinancing your mortgage for better rates or terms.

Upgrades and Renovations: Over time, consider which home improvements can both enhance your living experience and boost your property's value.

Sustainability: As the world becomes more environmentally conscious, think about how your home can contribute to this effort. Energy-efficient appliances, solar panels, or even a home garden can make a difference.

Potential Relocation: Life's unpredictability means that one day you might contemplate selling and relocating, whether for work, family, or simply a change of scenery. Knowing when and how to sell is just as vital as the buying process.

Parting Wisdom

Owning a home is more than just a financial investment; it's an investment in your future and a testament to your life's journey. Each crack you mend, every flower you plant, and all the memories you create within its walls contribute to your legacy.

Remember that every home, like its owner, has a unique story. As you pen the chapters of your own tale, may your home be a haven of joy, a source of pride, and a cornerstone of cherished moments.

Thank you for letting this guide be a part of your journey. Embrace the adventure of homeownership, for it is one of life's most rewarding experiences.

Glossary

Adjustable-Rate Mortgage (ARM): A type of mortgage where the interest rate can change (typically annually) based on a specific index.

Amortization: The process of paying off a loan over time through regular payments.

Appraisal: An evaluation of a property's market value, usually conducted by a licensed appraiser.

Assessment: A local tax levied against a property for a specific purpose.

Broker: A person or firm who is licensed to buy, sell, exchange, or lease real property for others for compensation.

Buyer's Agent: A real estate agent who represents only the buyer of a property in a transaction.

Capital Gains: The profit from the sale of a property or an investment.

Closing: The final step in a property sale when the title is transferred to the buyer, and funds are disbursed to the seller.

Closing Costs: Expenses, over and above the property price, that buyers and sellers incur to complete a real estate transaction.

Commission: The fee charged by a broker or agent for negotiating a real estate or loan transaction.

Condominium (Condo): Individual ownership of a unit in a multi-unit structure.

Contingency: A clause in a purchase agreement that specifies conditions that must be met.

Curb Appeal: How attractive the home appears from the street.

Deed: A legal document that proves ownership of a property.

Down Payment: The amount of money a buyer pays upfront to secure a property.

Easement: The right to use the land of another for a specific purpose.

Earnest Money: A deposit made by the potential home buyer to show they are serious.

Equity: The difference between a property's market value and the remaining amount on its mortgage.

Escrow: An account or arrangement where a third-party holds onto funds or documents.

Fair Market Value: The hypothetical price that a willing buyer and seller will agree upon.

FHA Loan: A loan insured by the Federal Housing Administration.

Fixed-Rate Mortgage: A type of mortgage where the interest rate remains consistent.

Foreclosure: The process by which a lender takes control of a property from a homeowner who has not made mortgage payments.

Homeowners Association (HOA): An organization in a subdivision or condo that makes and enforces rules for properties and residents.

Inspection: A physical examination of a property to determine its overall condition.

Lien: A legal claim against a property that must be paid when the property is sold.

Listing: A written contract that allows a real estate agent to represent a party in the sale.

Loan-to-Value (LTV): The ratio between the amount of a given mortgage loan and the total appraised value of the property.

Mortgage: A loan specifically used to purchase real estate.

Multiple Listing Service (MLS): A service used by real estate agents to view property listings.

Origination Fee: A fee paid to a lender for processing a new loan.

Points (or Discount Points): Prepaid interest on a mortgage loan.

Pre-Approval: A letter from a lender indicating how much they're willing to loan.

Principal: The amount borrowed for a loan.

Private Mortgage Insurance (PMI): Insurance compensating lenders if a borrower defaults.

Property Tax: A tax based on the value of a property, typically levied by local or municipal governments.

Seller's Agent (or Listing Agent): The real estate agent representing the property seller.

Short Sale: A sale in which the net proceeds fall short of the debts secured by liens against the property.

Survey: A drawing or map showing a property's boundaries and improvements.

Title: A legal document proving a person's rights to property possession.

Title Insurance: Insurance protecting from financial loss sustained from defects in a title.

Underwriting: The process of evaluating the risk of insuring a home loan.

VA Loan: A mortgage loan backed by the U.S. Department of Veterans Affairs.

Zoning: Municipal or local government laws dictating how particular geographic areas can be used.

This glossary offers a comprehensive overview of terms that are likely to be encountered in the realm of real estate. Always consult professionals or trusted sources if there are terms or concepts you're unsure about.

Checklists

The following pages can be filled in by you as you tour homes and conduct property inspections.

House Hunting Checklist for Home Buyers

Address: _____   Asking Price: _____

Neighborhood: _____   # of Bedrooms: ____ # of Bathrooms: ____

Year Build: _____ Annual Taxes: _____   Hoa Fee: _____ Sq Feet: _____

Walk Score: _____ Commute Time: _____ School District: _____

Exterior	Poor	Okay	Ideal
Roofs			
Gutters			
Driveway			
Front Doors			
Garbage door			
Curb Appeal			
Front Porch			
Back deck			
Side yard			
Fence			
Front Lawn			
Back lawn			
Landscape			

Foundation

cracked | chipped | water | n/a

Siding

brick | aluminum | shake | composite | unknown

Garage

___ car | attached | detached | storage | shop

Important notes/reminders

_____
_____
_____
_____
_____

Exterior	Poor	Okay	Ideal
Paint			
Ceiling			
Walls			
Moulding			
Kitchen			
Counter Space			
Cabinet Space			
Appliances			
Bathroom 1			
Bathroom 2			
Half bath			
Closet			
Bedroom 1			
Bedroom 2			
Master's bedroom			
Doors			
Windows			
Havc			
Furnace			
Laundry			
Basement			

Flooring Repair

___ kitchen   ___ bath   ___ rooms   ___ living room

Needs Repair

paint	Y	N	appliances	Y	N
flooring	Y	N	blinds	Y	N
roof	Y	N	plumbing	Y	N
electrical	Y	N	water/heater	Y	N

House Hunting Checklist for Home Buyers

Address: _____   Asking Price: _____

Neighborhood: _____   # of Bedrooms: ____ # of Bathrooms: ____

Year Build: _____   Annual Taxes: _____   Hoa Fee: _____ Sq Feet: _____

Walk Score: _____   Commute Time: _____   School District: _____

Exterior	Poor	Okay	Ideal
Roofs			
Gutters			
Driveway			
Front Doors			
Garbage door			
Curb Appeal			
Front Porch			
Back deck			
Side yard			
Fence			
Front Lawn			
Back lawn			
Landscape			

Foundation

cracked | chipped | water | n/a

Siding

brick | aluminum | shake | composite | unknown

Garage

___ car | attached | detached | storage | shop

Important notes/reminders

_____
_____
_____
_____
_____

Exterior	Poor	Okay	Ideal
Paint			
Ceiling			
Walls			
Moulding			
Kitchen			
Counter Space			
Cabinet Space			
Appliances			
Bathroom 1			
Bathroom 2			
Half bath			
Closet			
Bedroom 1			
Bedroom 2			
Master's bedroom			
Doors			
Windows			
Havc			
Furnace			
Laundry			
Basement			

Flooring Repair

___ kitchen   ___ bath   ___ rooms   ___ living room

Needs Repair

paint	Y	N	appliances	Y	N
flooring	Y	N	blinds	Y	N
roof	Y	N	plumbing	Y	N
electrical	Y	N	water/heater	Y	N

House Hunting Checklist for Home Buyers

Address: _____   Asking Price: _____

Neighborhood: _____   # of Bedrooms: ____ # of Bathrooms: ____

Year Build: _____   Annual Taxes: _____   Hoa Fee: _____   Sq Feet: _____

Walk Score: _____   Commute Time: _____   School District: _____

Exterior	Poor	Okay	Ideal
Roofs			
Gutters			
Driveway			
Front Doors			
Garbage door			
Curb Appeal			
Front Porch			
Back deck			
Side yard			
Fence			
Front Lawn			
Back lawn			
Landscape			

Foundation

cracked | chipped | water | n/a

Siding

brick | aluminum | shake | composite | unknown

Garage

___ car | attached | detached | storage | shop

Important notes/reminders

_____
_____
_____
_____
_____

Exterior	Poor	Okay	Ideal
Paint			
Ceiling			
Walls			
Moulding			
Kitchen			
Counter Space			
Cabinet Space			
Appliances			
Bathroom 1			
Bathroom 2			
Half bath			
Closet			
Bedroom 1			
Bedroom 2			
Master's bedroom			
Doors			
Windows			
Havc			
Furnace			
Laundry			
Basement			

Flooring Repair

___ kitchen   ___ bath   ___ rooms   ___ living room

Needs Repair

paint	Y	N	appliances	Y	N
flooring	Y	N	blinds	Y	N
roof	Y	N	plumbing	Y	N
electrical	Y	N	water/heater	Y	N

House Hunting Checklist for Home Buyers

Address: _____   Asking Price: _____
Neighborhood: _____   # of Bedrooms: ____ # of Bathrooms: ____
Year Build: _____ Annual Taxes: _____ Hoa Fee: _____ Sq Feet: _____
Walk Score: _____ Commute Time: _____ School District: _____

Exterior	Poor	Okay	Ideal	Exterior	Poor	Okay	Ideal
Roofs				Paint			
Gutters				Ceiling			
Driveway				Walls			
Front Doors				Moulding			
Garbage door				Kitchen			
Curb Appeal				Counter Space			
Front Porch				Cabinet Space			
Back deck				Appliances			
Side yard				Bathroom 1			
Fence				Bathroom 2			
Front Lawn				Half bath			
Back lawn				Closet			
Landscape				Bedroom 1			
				Bedroom 2			

Foundation

cracked | chipped | water | n/a

Siding

brick | aluminum | shake | composite | unknown

Garage

__ car | attached | detached | storage | shop

Exterior	Poor	Okay	Ideal
Master's bedroom			
Doors			
Windows			
Havc			
Furnace			
Laundry			
Basement			

Flooring Repair

___ kitchen ___ bath ___ rooms ___ living room

Needs Repair

paint	Y	N	appliances	Y	N
flooring	Y	N	blinds	Y	N
roof	Y	N	plumbing	Y	N
electrical	Y	N	water/heater	Y	N

Important notes/reminders

_____
_____
_____
_____
_____

House Hunting Checklist for Home Buyers

Address: _____   Asking Price: _____

Neighborhood: _____   # of Bedrooms: _____ # of Bathrooms: _____

Year Build: _____ Annual Taxes: _____   Hoa Fee: _____ Sq Feet: _____

Walk Score: _____ Commute Time: _____   School District: _____

Exterior	Poor	Okay	Ideal	Exterior	Poor	Okay	Ideal
Roofs				Paint			
Gutters				Ceiling			
Driveway				Walls			
Front Doors				Moulding			
Garbage door				Kitchen			
Curb Appeal				Counter Space			
Front Porch				Cabinet Space			
Back deck				Appliances			
Side yard				Bathroom 1			
Fence				Bathroom 2			
Front Lawn				Half bath			
Back lawn				Closet			
Landscape				Bedroom 1			
				Bedroom 2			
				Master's bedroom			
				Doors			
				Windows			
				Havc			
				Furnace			
				Laundry			
				Basement			

Foundation

cracked | chipped | water | n/a

Siding

brick | aluminum | shake | composite | unknown

Garage

___ car | attached | detached | storage | shop

Flooring Repair

___ kitchen   ___ bath   ___ rooms   ___ living room

Important notes/reminders

_____
_____
_____
_____

Needs Repair

paint	Y	N	appliances	Y	N
flooring	Y	N	blinds	Y	N
roof	Y	N	plumbing	Y	N
electrical	Y	N	water/heater	Y	N

Property Inspection Checklist

PROPERTY DETAILS

BEDROOMS		1	2	3	4
Flooring	Carpet				
	Floorboards				
	Tiles				
	Stained				
	Scratched				
	Cracks				
Walls	Paint				
	Wallpaper				
	Cracks				
	Damp patches				
Windows	Flyscreens				
	Blinds				
	Curtains				
	Lockable				
Balcony					
Ensuite					
Built-in wardrobe					
Air conditioning					
Ceiling fan					
Gas outlet					
TV aerial outlet					
Phone line					
Smoke alarm					
Number of power points					
Dimensions (metres)		x	x	x	x

BATHROOMS		1	2	3
Flooring	Tiles			
	Other			
	Cracks			
Walls	Tiles			
	Paint			
	Wallpaper			
	Cracks			
	Damp patches			
Windows	Flyscreens			
	Blinds			
	Curtains			
	Lockable			
Water pressure	High			
	Medium			
	Low			
Shower	Free standing			
	Over bath			
Bath				
Vanity				
Cupboards				
Towel rails				
Extraction fan				
Heater				
Toilet attached				
Number of power points				

NOTES

Property Inspection Checklist

PROPERTY DETAILS

BEDROOMS		1	2	3	4
Flooring	Carpet				
	Floorboards				
	Tiles				
	Stained				
	Scratched				
	Cracks				
Walls	Paint				
	Wallpaper				
	Cracks				
	Damp patches				
Windows	Flyscreens				
	Blinds				
	Curtains				
	Lockable				
Balcony					
Ensuite					
Built-in wardrobe					
Air conditioning					
Ceiling fan					
Gas outlet					
TV aerial outlet					
Phone line					
Smoke alarm					
Number of power points					
Dimensions (metres)		x	x	x	x

BATHROOMS		1	2	3
Flooring	Tiles			
	Other			
	Cracks			
Walls	Tiles			
	Paint			
	Wallpaper			
	Cracks			
	Damp patches			
Windows	Flyscreens			
	Blinds			
	Curtains			
	Lockable			
Water pressure	High			
	Medium			
	Low			
Shower	Free standing			
	Over bath			
Bath				
Vanity				
Cupboards				
Towel rails				
Extraction fan				
Heater				
Toilet attached				
Number of power points				

NOTES

Property Inspection Checklist

PROPERTY DETAILS

BEDROOMS		1	2	3	4
Flooring	Carpet				
	Floorboards				
	Tiles				
	Stained				
	Scratched				
	Cracks				
Walls	Paint				
	Wallpaper				
	Cracks				
	Damp patches				
Windows	Flyscreens				
	Blinds				
	Curtains				
	Lockable				
Balcony					
Ensuite					
Built-in wardrobe					
Air conditioning					
Ceiling fan					
Gas outlet					
TV aerial outlet					
Phone line					
Smoke alarm					
Number of power points					
Dimensions (metres)		x	x	x	x

BATHROOMS		1	2	3
Flooring	Tiles			
	Other			
	Cracks			
Walls	Tiles			
	Paint			
	Wallpaper			
	Cracks			
	Damp patches			
Windows	Flyscreens			
	Blinds			
	Curtains			
	Lockable			
Water pressure	High			
	Medium			
	Low			
Shower	Free standing			
	Over bath			
Bath				
Vanity				
Cupboards				
Towel rails				
Extraction fan				
Heater				
Toilet attached				
Number of power points				

NOTES

Property Inspection Checklist

PROPERTY DETAILS

BEDROOMS		1	2	3	4
Flooring	Carpet				
	Floorboards				
	Tiles				
	Stained				
	Scratched				
	Cracks				
Walls	Paint				
	Wallpaper				
	Cracks				
	Damp patches				
Windows	Flyscreens				
	Blinds				
	Curtains				
	Lockable				
Balcony					
Ensuite					
Built-in wardrobe					
Air conditioning					
Ceiling fan					
Gas outlet					
TV aerial outlet					
Phone line					
Smoke alarm					
Number of power points					
Dimensions (metres)		x	x	x	x

BATHROOMS		1	2	3
Flooring	Tiles			
	Other			
	Cracks			
Walls	Tiles			
	Paint			
	Wallpaper			
	Cracks			
	Damp patches			
Windows	Flyscreens			
	Blinds			
	Curtains			
	Lockable			
Water pressure	High			
	Medium			
	Low			
Shower	Free standing			
	Over bath			
Bath				
Vanity				
Cupboards				
Towel rails				
Extraction fan				
Heater				
Toilet attached				
Number of power points				

NOTES

Property Inspection Checklist

PROPERTY DETAILS

BEDROOMS

		1	2	3	4
Flooring	Carpet				
	Floorboards				
	Tiles				
	Stained				
	Scratched				
	Cracks				
Walls	Paint				
	Wallpaper				
	Cracks				
	Damp patches				
Windows	Flyscreens				
	Blinds				
	Curtains				
	Lockable				
Balcony					
Ensuite					
Built-in wardrobe					
Air conditioning					
Ceiling fan					
Gas outlet					
TV aerial outlet					
Phone line					
Smoke alarm					
Number of power points					
Dimensions (metres)		x	x	x	x

BATHROOMS

		1	2	3
Flooring	Tiles			
	Other			
	Cracks			
Walls	Tiles			
	Paint			
	Wallpaper			
	Cracks			
	Damp patches			
Windows	Flyscreens			
	Blinds			
	Curtains			
	Lockable			
Water pressure	High			
	Medium			
	Low			
Shower	Free standing			
	Over bath			
Bath				
Vanity				
Cupboards				
Towel rails				
Extraction fan				
Heater				
Toilet attached				
Number of power points				

NOTES